'TIL DEATH DO US PART

A Woman's Journey Through the 5 Stages of Widowhood and Life After

Sandie Fuenty

ISBN: 979-8-218-89719-2 (Paperback)

Book production by MysticqueRose Publishing Services LLC

Table of Contents

Dedication

This book is dedicated to the 51 years of married life I spent with my beloved husband, Jim (James William Fuenty). It is based on the war he fought in Vietnam and the war that he brought home with him (Agent Orange) and kept fighting until his battle ended on November 5, 2022. I learned what God's unconditional love is, in human form.

It is a remembrance of what Jim's life meant to me, and the love I feel for everyone that supported me throughout his illness and even now….our kids, our Sophia, my sister, my Mary Kay family. And to Latrice Jones, who invited me to write a story in her anthology, "Greatness is Your Journey", which led to this book. It started the healing process.

It is also dedicated to anyone who has lost a loved one, whether it be a tragic death or a long-term, caregiving death; may this book be a glimmer of hope and help you survive and walk through each new day with the knowledge that you are not alone.

Preface

Both Jim and I came from middle-income, hard-working parents. He grew up on the South Side of Chicago and was the second-oldest of 10 kids. I grew up in the suburbs of Chicago and had one sibling, my baby sister. My life was much more routine than his.

I did not know him before he enlisted in the Army, and didn't meet him until about a year and a half after he returned from Vietnam.

The Vietnam War was a "war" treated differently than any other in history. It wasn't just what happened overseas. It was what happened to people when they came home.

While the country was trying to figure out what it believed about Vietnam, the military was doing what it thought it needed to do to fight in a place like that, thick jungle, heat, terrain you couldn't see through. In the early 1960s, the U.S. began spraying Agent Orange and other herbicides over areas like the Mekong Delta to strip the jungle and expose supply routes along the Ho Chi Minh Trail. Back then, nobody was talking about long-term consequences. Years would pass before the toxic effects were uncovered, and even longer before people would admit what that meant for the men who were there.

By 1964 and 1965, everything escalated. Draft calls increased. Troop numbers grew. Bombing campaigns began. Teenagers were being sent into conditions they could not understand until they were already in them. Most of the guys who went were 17, 18, and 19. They were kids and had no idea what they were getting into.

When they came home, they received no parades, no hoorays, no recognition for what they endured. They were spit on. They were judged. People acted like they had chosen the war, when many of them were simply trying to do what they believed was their patriotic duty. They came back and were expected to drop right into "real life," with no real debriefing, no help, no understanding, and no room to say what they had seen.

Jim enlisted on March 10, 1964, when he was 17 years old. His parents had to sign for him to be able to join the Army. He was honorably discharged on January 30, 1967. He was assigned to D Troop, 1st Squadron, 1st Cavalry, 1st Armored Division at Fort Hood. I do not know what all that means. We have tried researching for information, but the different logistics areas were combined and ceased to exist over the years.

Jim went over to Vietnam in August of 1965, and he went by freighter. He was not one of the "lucky" ones who were flown over. I remember stories of 23 days at sea, and they would fight to find space on the deck to sleep and avoid the disgusting smells down below of vomit and bodily functions. He landed in Da Nang and was then transported to Pleiku and An Khe.

What he faced there we will never know because, like so many others, when he came back, he did not talk about Vietnam or his experiences. The memories were put in the far darkest spot of his mind. We know so little about what he was forced to do or witness.

But I do know this: Vietnam explained so much about him.

He trusted no one. He had all the effects of PTSD but would not acknowledge it. He was very volatile, and he had built up a strong wall against people and relationships. Little did we know this would be the slow, progressive death he would be facing years later as Agent Orange attacked his body.

Please note that children and grandchildren are still being affected by this exposure that the soldiers experienced.

Before I knew him, while he was over there fighting and staying alive, I was here in the US, still in High School, hearing about Vietnam occasionally on the news, and corresponding with a couple of friends who were there. No one ever wrote about what was really going on.

Approximately a year and a half after he returned, we met. We dated for about two years before we were married on August 1st, 1971. Our lives were entwined for 51 plus years of marriage.

For a long time, it felt like the war was behind us because it was behind him, locked away. But the body doesn't forget what the mind tries to bury. The illnesses came later, and they came steadily, like a long chain reaction that nobody could stop.

It took till the early 1990s for the VA to recognize the repercussions of Agent Orange and to start compiling information on the Agent Orange Registry. By then, many families had already been living with the consequences for years.

Jim was a fighter with his health and everything. He fought up until the last week or so of his life. He was still fighting a battle. He passed away peacefully on November 5th, 2022.

I have written stories for anthologies before, but when a friend asked me if I'd like to write a story in her anthology, and I said yes, the only thing that kept coming to mind to write about was grief. In a book that was going to be about uplifting and encouraging stories, I wasn't sure how grief could fit in it. But it did, and not in a depressing way. It was a story of what's possible.

Once I finished that story, I knew I needed to tell people what I went through and what I learned along the way. I had no idea how to start.

But in God's perfect timing, a week later, I was at a women's conference and met Porsché and heard her speak. That's when I really knew it was going to get done.

I must say that writing a book is like reliving that period of time, dissecting it in a way I never would have done if this were not a passion to finish. When you are in the midst of life, you don't realize what you are not feeling, seeing, or acknowledging. So much of that came during the painful, but healing, pulling out of these emotions and memories that were pushed away.

I must also say thank you to Porsché because she was there with me, listening to me ramble, sniff, laugh, live through the memories again, and she kept me on track of what I needed to do.

If this book helps one more person be able to wake up tomorrow morning and say, "I know I'm not alone. I will just take God's hand and allow Him to lead me through today," then I know it was worth all the tears and draining tiredness it required to get it down on paper.

~ Sandie Fuenty

S. g. Fuenty

Introduction

I walked into a new doctor's office at the beginning of the year. As I entered, I noticed how clean and organized everything was. The front office personnel who were smiling as I walked in, the perfectly stacked brochures on the front desk, even the comfortable gray leather couches that filled the space, all seemed perfectly aligned.

I found it oddly comforting, given the recent chaos and heartache I was experiencing.

Despite the beauty of the office, the feeling of confusion and frustration rested heavily in my gut. The front desk handed me the dreaded clipboard with all the New Patient forms to fill out…never a welcome chore to try and fit your life into little boxes and lines.

I sat on one of the couches, crossed my leg over my knee, and began the task. I was doing fine until I got to the part about marital status; you know the one — single, married, divorced, widowed.

I stopped.

Never before had I realized that I was now a widow and must check that box.

As I sat in silence with tears welling up, I didn't want to answer it because somehow that would be one more step I had to take to admitting that I was a widow and he was no longer here.

I was used to being in doctors' offices all the time, whether it was emergency rooms, the VA hospital, or the many scheduled doctor appointments. Needless to say, I was no stranger to filling out these forms. But this was different. This was me, by myself, having to answer for myself.

Jim was no longer here, but somehow, I hadn't fully taken that in.

As I sat staring at that box, I reflected on the recent emotional roller coaster of his death.

At first, it was relief.

It felt strange to remember that I was relieved after he was gone. He had suffered so long after being exposed to Agent Orange back during the Vietnam War. Because of this, he ended up with a never-ending list of sicknesses, diseases, and ailments, so I was glad that he finally found peace.

But after relief came an intense wave of guilt. "Why would I be relieved that my husband of 51 years was gone?" But I didn't sit with the guilt long, as numbness and even denial started to take over. This was all so new to me; these emotions and realizations that I had kept in check and locked away inside of me.

Over time, I have come to know that there are five stages that I went through; some very separately, some overlapping. I can look back now and see how the order makes sense. At that time, I didn't even recognize what they were.

I call them the 5 Stages of Widowhood:

1. Relief
2. Guilt
3. Numbness
4. Letting Go
5. Rebuilding

I realize it might not be the same for everybody. Perhaps the order is shifted for you, or perhaps there was a stage that you experienced that's totally unique to you. Nonetheless, these five main stages showed up forcefully as I journeyed through widowhood.

But it wasn't some spontaneous revelation. I didn't wake up one morning and suddenly realize that I'd gone through these five stages. In actuality, I became present to them as I made my way through a series of lessons.

With each passing day and each new experience, I learned something new, powerful, and sometimes painful. That's why I decided to write this book. It was a series of lessons that allowed me to understand the stages that I was going through.

I didn't realize at the time that I would find myself in a world of lessons as a widow. Who knew that there would be a learning curve to this?

But there I was, with the clipboard on my lap, recounting the lessons I've learned along the way; how my family taught me strength, how advocacy and my trust in God would play a pivotal role in healing, and of course, how I could continue to love after death.

My intent with this book is to pass on to you the lessons that I learned the hard way. You will learn how I climbed those mountains, how I reclaimed my identity but still honored my husband and our marriage, and how you can do the same.

After reading through the lessons and stories, you'll dive deeper into the *5 Stages of Widowhood* and how they showed up for me. As you read, you may discover where you are within the five stages and perhaps gain clarity, support, and the ability to finally exhale.

I pray that you receive hope through your journey of widowhood and understand that others are on this journey with you.

It's funny how I always pictured widows as mostly old people, hobbling around and needing help.

Here I am at 76, and I do not fit that stereotype. For the first time in my life, I am completely on my own, with no one who could tell me what to do each day. Our lives had become such a medical routine that I never had to give it much thought. Did he have a doctor's appointment or not? Did he need to have special medication that day? Those were the questions that filled my life, but now I am on the other side with a new life to get used to.

This book will take you to where I had to check the "W" box…the heartbreaks, the strength, the mindless routines, the love, the learning what is really important; 51 years of marriage and learning what love really is. You will be able to meet Jim, our family, friends, the doctors, and all the angels God placed in our paths. You will also learn a little about the Vietnam War and Agent Orange, and what the servicemen and women who returned home brought with them. My intent is that you will learn about how I coped (or didn't), you'll dry a few tears with me, and that you'll find your own way to deal with this journey.

There will be rough days, but there will be days when you see the sun shining gloriously again.

I promise that by the time you finish reading this book, you will not feel alone.

CHAPTER 1

The Power of Children

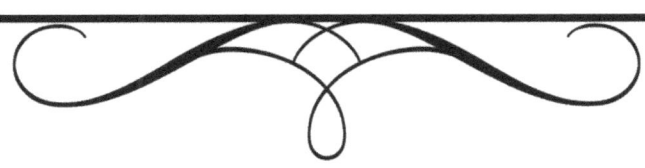

We often believe that, as parents, we're meant to be strong for our children, especially in times of need or distress. I've always felt this way about our kids. But one of the most profound lessons I learned, as Jim's health continued to decline and I began to enter widowhood, was that, at some point, our children would soon be the ones doing the protecting and saving.

We were blessed with two children and two grandchildren; Jimmy (our oldest), Lindsey (our daughter), and our grandbabies (Jimmy's daughters), Sophia and Penelope ("PJ"). Surprisingly, it was our granddaughter, Sophia, who became one of my rocks.

Sophia was six years old throughout most of Jim's illness. Without the need for much explanation, she knew there were things that her PaPa couldn't do with her like he used to, but she didn't seem to mind.

Her ability to embrace things simply as they were astounded me. No questions. No worries. No judgement. She simply accepted things for what they were.

I remember moments when she and her PaPa would swordfight.

In the front room of our home, Jim was seated in his recliner, the recliner that served as both his bed and chair. Sophia, with her usual bubbly self, ran around Jim, inciting trouble.

She was on a mission: to challenge her PaPa to a head-to-head duel.

Armed with empty wrapping paper rolls, Jim and Sophia began to fight. Squeals of laughter burst from Sophia as she batted at PaPa's "sword". Jim would come to life as he leaned forward in his chair to combat his tiny opponent. On and on the battle went until the rolls began to fall apart. Even with broken swords, the duel continued all the way until Sophia came just close enough to be grabbed by Jim for an intense tummy tickle session. Her laugh and squeals filled the house.

These moments were quite common. So much so, that Sophia eventually began to call her PaPa "Ticklebelly".

As time went on, and Jim's health declined further, Sophia's love grew. Never was she fazed by the progression of his illness. She would make him cards and draw pictures to cheer him up while he was in the hospital. But what took me aback was that her pictures were a blend of reality and imagination. She would draw him in a hospital gown, taking her to a carnival. Another picture showed them together with him on his crutches, and he only had half of one leg.

She missed him but wasn't hurt by any of it.

We lived about an hour away from our son and daughter, Jimmy and Lindsey, who shared a house. After the first amputation, we stayed with them for several days and eventually went back home. After the second amputation, we found ourselves staying more often because it was closer to Jim's doctors and hospitals. Around June of 2022, me, Jim, and our two dogs, moved into their living room with a hospital bed and lift chair, with every intention of someday moving back to our home. I would go home every three to four days to freshen the cats' food and water, clean the litter, and love on them. It was also a time when I could be by myself and disconnect before heading back.

Sophia was right in the middle of it all and understood that when the firemen and paramedics came for PaPa, she should stay in her room till they had him ready to leave. Nonetheless, she was always so excited when he'd get better and be able to come back "home".

After each long day at the hospital, I would return to the kids' house and literally fall into bed with my clothes on, passing out from exhaustion. Sometimes I'd manage a bite or two of dinner with them, but reliving the day's medical updates was hard - repeating what the doctors said about Jim's condition.

But then there was Sophia - my little ray of sunshine. Every morning, she would quietly peek into my room, checking to see if I was awake. She'd come close, give me a gentle hug, and ask about PaPa. "How's PaPa doing?" she'd say, her small voice filled with concern. And then, just as quickly, she'd be off to school.

Those moments were my lifeline. Her simple act of checking on me, of showing she cared, would signal that it was time to get moving again. I'd get up, feed the dogs, take a shower, eat something, and head back to the hospital. Jim would be waiting, anxiously listening for my footsteps down the hallway.

Sophia was like a little soldier in our war against illness - supporting me, keeping me going when I thought I couldn't. She was just a child, but she understood more than most adults would. Her morning ritual was more than just a routine; it was her way of taking care of me, of making sure I was okay.

In those dark days, Sophia was my strength, my reminder that life continues, that there's still love and hope, even in the midst of uncertainty.

It's a blessing to see Jim live on through his granddaughters. Their pride and love for him have given me strength and comfort.

While Sophia began to open my eyes to the power I was realizing I needed, it was my own children who truly solidified the lesson that our kids have the utmost strength.

Jimmy and Lindsey were truly my rocks.

Jimmy's love and power were what I needed to ensure I remained logical. He was the one who would ask the technical questions and procedures, and document what the doctors said.

There's one moment in particular that solidified Jimmy's strength in my mind.

In the later days of Jim's illness, we were constantly at the hospital. During one of those stays, Jim struggled with finding something to watch on the room's television. He seemed to spend an eternity flicking through the channels to find something that would hold his interest. I watched him as he repeatedly pressed the "Up" button in frustration. Watching his annoyance grow, Jimmy decided enough was enough.

Without saying a word, he ripped out a piece of paper from a notebook we kept nearby. He made two columns on the page and gently reached for the remote. With a slight frown on Jim's face, he released the remote, and his son went to work.

Rapidly clicking and writing, Jimmy noted all the channels that would be of interest to his father. Soon, he had a page with the names and numbers of the channels; a veritable cheat sheet for his old man.

He handed over the sheet and the remote back to Jim, who received it with a quiet, acknowledging nod.

I watched in awe as Jimmy stayed quiet through the whole process. He sat back in his chair as calmly as could be, not awaiting a 'Thank you" or any form of gratitude.

But that's Jimmy; forever the problem solver without requiring recognition.

I knew right then and there that our boy was going to be able to help me remain on firm ground even when the inevitable would happen.

Just as Jimmy was the rock for my mind, Lindsey was the rock for my heart.

She and her brother are complete opposites, but both have the strength of their father.

Lindsey is six years younger than her brother and always kept us on our toes. She was the one who would get caught sneaking in the house through the doggy door as a teenager, hoping her dad wouldn't see her.

During Jim's toughest moments, Lindsey took off six months from work to be able to be present for his care. But that kind of "springing into action" was second-nature for her. Lindsey never needed tons of explanation before jumping in to help on her own.

Like father, like daughter.

Even in the thick of it, Lindsey would do whatever was required. There was a time when she was alone during one of Jim's "episodes".

I was out feeding the cats when Lindsey called me, her voice filled with panic. She was using Jim's phone, and I could tell something was wrong. Jim was having one of his episodes - those mysterious moments where he would just... disappear. It wasn't like a normal fainting spell; he was completely gone.

This was about the eighth time something like this had happened. Doctors kept trying to explain it away as low blood pressure or low sugar, but we knew it was something more. This time, Lindsey was alone in the house when it occurred.

She immediately called the paramedics and stayed incredibly calm. They kept her on the phone, asking her to check on Jim constantly. She had to report whether he was breathing, if he was responding - all while being completely alone. I was miles away, and she was managing everything.

Those ten minutes on the phone felt like an eternity. When the paramedics arrived, they wouldn't let her ride with them to the hospital. They even warned her that she probably wouldn't be allowed in, not even me. She was so desperate that she drove to the hospital and sat outside, hoping to find a way to be near him.

Lindsey was stoic, following instructions perfectly while managing her internal fear. She held onto Jim, made sure he knew she was there, and handled the entire terrifying situation with remarkable strength. It was in that moment that I truly saw how much of her father she was - calm, precise, and incredibly brave in a crisis.

Sometimes, when the sunset paints the sky in Jim's favorite colors, Lindsey and I will look at each other and just know. We'll whisper something, maybe a joke Jim would have loved, and suddenly there'll be a random noise - like a creak or a rustle - and we'll both pause. "I hope you didn't hear that, Dad," one of us will say, and then we'll burst out laughing.

These moments are our connection. They're how we keep Jim alive between us. We can talk about him, laugh about memories, and feel his presence in the most unexpected ways. When a strange sound happens right after we mention him, we'll exchange a knowing look. It's like he's still here, still listening, still part of our conversation.

After losing Jim, these moments with Lindsey have been my lifeline. She understands my grief without me having to explain it. We can sit in silence or break into spontaneous laughter, and it all feels right. She carries so much of her father in her - not just his strength, but his spirit, his ability to make light of serious moments.

When the world feels too heavy, Lindsey anchors me. She reminds me that love doesn't end with loss; it transforms. And in those quiet, magical moments when we feel Jim's presence, my heart feels whole again.

When you lose someone, especially your partner, you think you need to be strong. You believe you have to protect everyone around you, shield them from the pain. But what I learned is that sometimes, it's the other way around. Your family - especially your children - they're the ones holding you up, keeping you moving forward.

It's not about grand gestures or profound moments of healing. It's about the small things. A phone call. A hug. A simple "How are you doing?" A child peeking into your room, making sure you're okay. These tiny acts of love are what truly sustain you.

I discovered that my children understood more than I ever gave them credit for. They knew exactly what I needed, often before I did. They became my anchors, my lifelines. Lindsey, with her ability to make me laugh even in the darkest moments. Sophia, with her morning check-ins that reminded me that life continues. Jimmy, with his logical mind and silent actions.

My advice to you: Let them in. Let your family support you. Don't try to be a hero. Those little reminders that they know what you're going through, that they're here to help make everything doable - those are what will carry you through.

You might be surprised to find that you need your children more than they need you, and that's okay. Grief isn't a journey you take alone. It's a path you walk together, step by step, moment by moment, supported by the love that surrounds you.

CHAPTER 2

"I didn't sign up for this."

When we get married and say "I do," we actually have no idea what we are saying "I do" to. When we repeat the words "for better or worse, in sickness and in health," do we really understand what that will require of us? No one stands at the altar imagining wheelchairs, amputations, insulin pumps, or becoming a nurse in their own living room.

But life has a way of handing us the unimagined.

Jim and I both had been married before (briefly), so maybe we had a little more realism than most first-timers. But still, nothing could have prepared me.

Jim was quiet when I met him, still carrying the weight of Vietnam, walls built high around him. Somehow, I slipped through those walls. We dated for two years, then on a dare, and to save an eight-dollar license fee, we drove from Chicago to Las Vegas in a '71 MG Midget and got married in the Little White Chapel. His parents were our witnesses. We were young, fearless, and thought we could handle anything.

We didn't know what we were signing up for, though.

At first, the vow of "in sickness and in health" was mine to carry. I had major surgery to remove almost all of my colon, leaving me with an ileostomy bag. Jim became my nurse, tending to me, even joking about it in public by calling it "my buddy." That was his way: using humor to soften the hard edges. Later, as his health began to fail, the roles reversed and the humor became one of our survival tools.

But here's what I didn't expect: becoming my husband's caretaker in the most physical, intimate ways. Helping him down the hall to the bathroom. Lifting him in and out of a wheelchair. Holding his body steady over a commode placed next to his recliner because walking across the house was no longer possible. Sometimes I honestly couldn't tell who it drained more, him or me. These were the moments when my heart whispered, *I didn't sign up for this.*

Yet, something in me shifted. Slowly, I realized: it doesn't matter.

It didn't matter how frustrating it was to cook meals he wouldn't eat, or to throw away pots of food that went untouched because by the time it was ready, it no longer appealed to him. It didn't matter that his body betrayed him daily in ways I couldn't fix, no matter how hard I tried. It didn't matter that I was exhausted, angry, or scared at times. What mattered was that he was still here, and that I loved him.

There was a day I finally reached my breaking point. I remember standing in the kitchen, overwhelmed by medications, numbers, nutrition charts, and rules I couldn't seem to get right. I had tried to force him to eat better, to take what he needed, to follow what the doctors prescribed, but none of it worked the way it was supposed to. His body simply wouldn't cooperate. That was the day I handed it over to God. I told myself: *I can't fix this. I can't carry both his illness and my own frustration. My role is to love him, not to save him.* That shift kept me sane.

As his care got more complicated, we each fell into our own roles. While we stayed at the kids' house, Jimmy played sports on TV to keep Jim engaged. Sophia would grab her microphone and put on full concerts just for her PaPa. Lindsey and I learned to administer IV antibiotics at home…twice. Jim had a PICC (Peripherally Inserted Central Catheter) line, and we became nurses overnight. I was the only one he'd let clean his bedsores at first. Later, he let the kids help, too. That alone showed how much he was letting go, how much he trusted them.

Still, nothing about it was linear. One minute, we were hearing from the doctors that things were improving. Next, we were being told to prepare for the worst. Then we'd get another glimmer of hope. It was exhausting, that constant up and down. When he was transferred to a long-term acute care facility, we thought maybe he was turning a corner. I remember him using a wheelchair for the first time on his own and telling me, "You'll probably end up doing most of the pushing...until I get my electric chair." We laughed. He still had that spark.

And then, he coded, though they were able to bring him back. After that, everything changed.

The reality we had to face was that this could be the end, that he wasn't going to get better. Our lives had been on a constant roller coaster for the last six months, yet we found ourselves clinging to the hope that he would prove the doctors wrong one more time and surprise them with his recovery.

Yet, it became harder and harder to stay positive. The VA was indeed giving him the best care possible and did test after test to try to help him, but his body was so fragile that at a certain point it could no longer listen to him saying "fight". He had been a fighter throughout our marriage, not physical fighting but the mental kind, where he refused to give up. When he started realizing things were really getting serious for him, he spoke with conviction and said, "I want to fight. I don't want to die". So we did as he asked and kept fighting the doctors and his health along with him.

It became an emotional battle with lots of ups and downs. After the intubation tube was removed, we had been warned, yet again, that he could slip away within a couple of hours. We knew the facts, but refused to give in. Despite what the doctors projected, Jim lasted another week and a half with his mind and spirit intact. His brain, his ability to recognize us, and even his communication with us (although limited and without words), were showing us that he was still inside that body and fully alert. Once he got home with Hospice, he was able to stop fighting and finally rest completely.

I wouldn't trade those last few months for anything, though. They were hard, unimaginable at times, but they gave the kids a chance to see a different side of their dad, a softer, more vulnerable side, and Jim let them love on him in a way he never had before. He needed them, and they were there for him completely.

So what advice would I give to anyone who finds themselves in this place, staring down all the things you never signed up for?

First, let go of the illusion that you can control it. You cannot fix them. You cannot make their body do what it will not do. Your responsibility is love, not cure.

Second, let them keep their dignity as long as possible. Let them do what they can, while they can, even if it's slower, messier, or imperfect.

Third, don't carry their limitations as your own failures. Their illness is not your fault. Their inability is not your inadequacy.

Finally, remember why you said "I do" in the first place. It wasn't because you had a contract with perfect circumstances. It was because of love; love that holds steady in good times and bad, in sickness and health.

No, I didn't know what I was signing up for and neither did he. But after all those years, the truth is this: it didn't matter.

CHAPTER 3

To Love is to Advocate

Sometimes when I look back on Jim's battle after the war, I am reminded of certain life skills that I was forced to improve. Being a mother or wife, I believe we all, at some point, find ourselves protecting our loved ones. So something like advocacy was not new to me, but I never thought my ability to advocate for my husband would be a matter of life and death.

I learned early on that it is so important to be fully informed about the medical treatments and prescriptions your loved one is receiving. You need to ask questions, even when you're tired, confused, or overwhelmed; you must ask anyway. Doctors might be using words you don't understand, the nurses may be busy, and the patient (your loved one) might not be fully tracking what's happening. Jim certainly wasn't. Every time they asked how he was feeling, he'd just say, "Fine," but we knew that wasn't true.

There were times when new medications were added to his long list of 30+ prescriptions, and even I struggled to keep track; when to give what, what not to mix, what he was allowed to eat or drink. It became like managing a chemistry lab, and if something was missed or misunderstood, it could be dangerous. One mistake could cost everything.

I'll never forget the time Jim started acting strange. For several days, he was saying things that didn't make sense. He was hallucinating, talking about little bunnies running under the TV stand and warning us to be careful not to step on them, but the way he said it, it was serious. He believed it. He also kept talking about two children, Noel and Jackson, and was deeply concerned about keeping them safe, handing them to us like they were real. He'd instruct us on how to hold them and how to cover them properly. It was truly heartbreaking.

At first, we humored him, thinking maybe it was just exhaustion or stress. He didn't have a fever, and physically, everything seemed the same. But then one morning, he had another one of his "episodes," and we called the paramedics. After a long day in the ER, the doctors finally diagnosed him with *drug-induced encephalopathy*, a serious brain dysfunction caused by a bad interaction between an antibiotic and one of his pain medications. He was, in plain terms, higher than a kite, and nobody had caught it. A few days in the hospital getting the medications out of his system, and thankfully, he came home.

But that should've never happened.

After that, we made it a rule; any time a new medication was introduced, we asked: "Are there any possible interactions with what he's already taking?" We refused to assume anyone had double-checked, because the truth is, sometimes they haven't.

It's not about pointing fingers; it's about protecting the one you love.

We learned that we often knew more about Jim's day-to-day condition than the doctors did. They might only look at the chart notes that applied to their specialty. They'd skim for what mattered to them, not necessarily what mattered to us. One of the worst questions a doctor could ask at the VA was, "And what are you here for today?" That question would send Jim into a quiet storm. He'd shut down completely. That's when I'd step in and explain everything: why we were there, what he was experiencing, and what had changed.

There's a moment I still carry with me, one that changed how I see caregiving and advocacy. After Jim's second amputation, when we were finally home again, I thought we were on the road to healing, but the relief was short-lived. The VA had written his orders for a specific brand of wound cleanser and sent us home with it to use. When the home health nurse came, she refused to use what we had been given. "I can only follow the orders exactly," she said. She stated that she was instructed to use simple "saline" and not any branded products; thus, no product would be used. What was crazy was that both the branded cleanser and the generic saline had the same purpose, but unfortunately, different labels, and that stalled everything. I begged her, explaining that this was what the VA hospital instructed us to use and that I was already worried about the way Jim's foot was looking, but she stood firm.

To make matters worse, there had already been confusion transferring Jim's care after we moved back to our home, so visits were delayed longer than the usual two or three days. I was suspicious that something wasn't right. I had even taken photos of his foot to send to the doctors, but by the time a different nurse came and unwrapped the bandage, the infection had spread too far.

Earlier, another nurse had mistakenly sealed his two remaining toes inside the wound vac seal. She insisted it would be fine, but I'll never forget watching those toes wither until they turned black. That mistake cost Jim even more of his foot. The next time we went in, they admitted him immediately and told us a below-the-knee amputation was the only option. Jim shook his head and muttered, "Why didn't they just do this the first time so we didn't have to go through all of this?"

I can't explain the helplessness I felt in those days. Every delay, every rigid rule, every mistake, all piled up and I couldn't undo it. If Jim hadn't been so stubborn, I would have thrown him in the car and driven straight to the VA emergency room myself. Looking back, maybe that's what I should have done.

What I've learned since then is that as a caregiver, you cannot sit quietly on the sidelines. In these moments, you become the bridge. You are the one connecting the dots between what's best for them and what's being offered. That's what it means to advocate.

Even small things required speaking up. During one of Jim's last hospital stays, he wasn't allowed to eat or drink, not even ice chips. Our daughter Lindsey went out into the hallway, hoping to find one of the doctors. As fate would have it, several of them were standing together discussing Jim's condition. She marched right up and asked why he couldn't at least have ice chips. They explained the risk of him aspirating.

Her response?

"Well... what better place to be if something happens? Can't we at least try?"

They looked at each other, and finally, they agreed. They gave her a cup of ice chips to take back to her dad. He lit up like a Christmas tree. It had become a running joke with the nurses. Whenever they'd ask if he needed anything, he'd say, very slowly and deliberately, "Waaater." It was a small victory for him.

Lindsey was his advocate that day, and many others. She's the one who pushed to get him home when we knew the end was near. The doctors were hesitant. They didn't think he was stable enough to make the trip. But we kept asking, "What difference does it make where it happens? All he wants is to be home."

Eventually, they agreed. They arranged the ambulance, the hospital bed, the hospice medication, all of it. And when we told him it was happening, he just kept mouthing the word, "Home."

He arrived on a Friday afternoon. We got him comfortable. We surrounded him with love. And by the next morning, he had slipped away peacefully.

He didn't die in a hospital. He died the way he wanted to, in his home with his family, and we fought for that.

That's the power of advocacy. If we had stayed silent, if we had just nodded and accepted everything as it came, Jim would've died in a hospital bed, with fluorescent lights and beeping machines, instead of in his living room with his family.

But there's another side to advocacy that I need to talk about.

You have to remember: doctors and nurses are human too. We had one doctor that I ended up riding the elevator with after a long day. I asked him a few questions, and he paused. Then he said something I'll never forget. He told me he was going through something similar at home with his own dad. That they were struggling to make decisions, trying their best, but nothing was clear. In that moment, I saw him not just as a doctor, but as a son.

We want to believe our loved one is the only patient that matters. But the truth is, these professionals are often juggling multiple cases, long hours, and their own personal lives. That doesn't excuse anything, but it does help you approach them with compassion. Just as we're doing our best, so are they.

There were doctors who barely looked up from their clipboards, but there were others like Dr. Khan, who sat there quietly thinking through options, who cared deeply, and who considered every angle. He was the one who refused to operate on Jim's gallbladder. He said it was too risky, but we didn't want to hear that, although we respected him for it. He could've pushed ahead just to say he tried, but instead, he made the hard call to protect what was left of Jim's strength.

There was also the radiology tech who had taken Jim for X-rays on several different ER visits, who asked if he could pray with

Jim before taking him in for scans. It caught us off guard. We weren't expecting that. Jim was not a religious man, so we didn't know how he would react, but he agreed, and in that small moment, there was peace. Science and spirit met, and it helped.

Those moments reminded me that *we're not the only advocates.* Sometimes, others are advocating for our loved ones too, in ways we don't always see right away.

So don't just be willing to fight for your person. Be willing to receive support from those who are fighting alongside you. Speak up. Ask questions. Push back when something feels off. But also, stay open to compassion, teamwork, and quiet prayers from unexpected places.

CHAPTER 4

Knowledge Is Invaluable

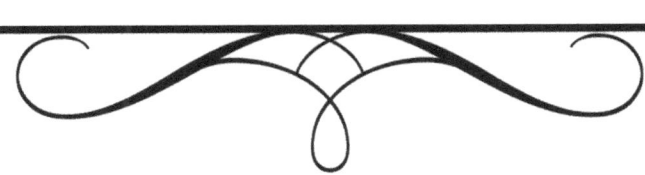

oesn't it seem like every person you come across has a solution to your problem? Or they feel like they know exactly how to fix the dilemma you're going through?

When you're walking through illness, caregiving, or even experiencing grief, people love to offer advice. While most of them mean well, I've learned this: listen with open ears and an open heart, but take it all with a grain of salt.

The best advice comes from those who've actually lived it simply because experience is the best teacher. You'll hear a lot of, "Well, my uncle had this," or "My coworker said that," but if the information isn't factual, if it's not something you can verify, don't act on it. Your decisions, especially when it comes to health, need to be grounded in truth, not hearsay.

It seems like a lifetime ago now, but I still remember when my sister's late husband, Henryk, told us to make sure Jim got on the Agent Orange Registry at the VA. At the time, we weren't connected with the VA and we hadn't even heard of the registry. That, on top of everyone else offering all sorts of advice that didn't quite resonate, caused us to let Henryk's advice slide initially.

Like Jim, Henryk was also a Vietnam veteran. He could be gruff, irritable, and rough around the edges, but over the years,

I've come to understand him better. The more I learn about what those men went through, the more I get it.

Henryk had been having health issues, and eventually, they diagnosed him with a brain tumor. The treatments didn't help, and within six months, he was gone. His doctors believed the tumor was related to Agent Orange exposure. That shook us, but it also made us take his advice seriously.

If we hadn't listened to him, I truly don't know what the next 20 years of Jim's care would have looked like. Jim was still relatively healthy back then, maybe just some high blood pressure, so it didn't feel urgent, but Henryk insisted, and thank God he did. Every single one of those VA benefits became a lifeline.

Because we got Jim on the Registry, everything changed. All of his medical care became covered, and as time went on and his health got worse, that coverage became more than helpful. It became life-sustaining; medications, hospital stays, surgeries, transportation, meals on Veterans Day, and even access to doctors who actually *understood* what he was going through. It wasn't just the physical care either. There was something about being in that VA community that mattered, too. These people understood all the behind-the-scenes issues that we couldn't even fathom. That one piece of advice, at Henryk's insistence, made a world of difference.

I think some of the best lessons we learned came from simply sitting in those VA waiting rooms. Watching. Listening. I learned more about the Vietnam War from hearing other veterans talk than I ever did from a textbook. Their stories, their struggles, and their wisdom were like free education if you were willing to pay attention. That taught me early on: pick the brains of survivors, ask questions, and do your research. Understanding what your loved one is facing makes a huge difference.

Funny enough, though, when it came to widowhood itself, the knowledge wasn't so easy to come by.

After Jim passed, there was no Henryk waiting with the next helpful tip. There were no clear answers and no roadmap. The support just wasn't there. I expected someone, somewhere, to help guide me through it, but nothing really prepares you. People didn't know what to say. Even my closest friends seemed unsure. Do they bring him up? Do they stay quiet?

I remember going to a women's group two weeks after Jim died. It was my birthday. I showed up because I figured, *Why not?* It was something familiar and something normal. But when I walked into that room, it was like everyone froze. You could feel the awkwardness. People didn't know whether to say something or stay quiet. They didn't want to make it worse, but didn't know how to make it better either. I could tell they cared. I already knew that, but still, no one really knew how to show it.

People simply don't talk about widowhood. They don't know how. Even my closest friends didn't know what to say, and that silence can be deafening.

The VA gave me a stack of brochures about survivor benefits.

Fill out this form.
Call this number.
Apply for this.

I did, but there was nothing about *how* to walk through the grief. No emotional roadmap, no warning signs for the sleepless nights, the loneliness in broad daylight, or the identity shift that comes after losing your partner of over 50 years. I had to figure all that out on my own.

Eventually, I found an online group of Vietnam veteran widows. That became a place where I could listen and learn. Some of those women have no life outside of their husbands, and they are still suffering. Others have leaned into their faith, their families, and their hobbies. They've found ways to stay connected to life.

Watching them taught me something important: you still have a choice even in grief. You can get stuck or you can move forward. I chose to keep living.

I also started reading books. *The Women* by Kristin Hannah really stuck with me. Even though it was fiction, it opened up a different perspective about Vietnam and the emotional toll it took on both the men and the women. Another one, *Home Before Morning* by Lynda Van Devanter, was written by a nurse who served during the war, and it helped me understand even more. These weren't widowhood books per se, but they gave me context. They helped me see my story in a bigger picture.

But even with those books, even with the widows group, I can still say: there's not enough out there.

Grief is so often tucked away, not talked about, and not addressed. We need more spaces to be honest about what this journey is, and we need more people to share what they've learned. The truth is, what you don't know *can* hurt you.

Looking back, I think what helped me most was what I *did* know: what Henryk told us, what I picked up from watching other widows, or reading those books. But I also know there were things I wish someone had said to me early on, so I didn't have to figure out the hard way.

Sometimes I find myself thinking that perhaps I'm not the stereotypical widow whose pain drives her daily thoughts and actions. I've always been pretty resilient. I've been through hard times before, and I've come out the other side. Even with that, I wish someone had warned me about how anticipatory grief, grieving while they're still alive, is a real thing. It's heavy, and when death finally comes, it can feel more like a release than a shock. You finally exhale. The book closes. You get to put down the weight you've been carrying for so long.

Yet, I know this would have been a lot harder if I hadn't had people like Henryk, if I hadn't had those little slivers of knowledge along the way.

Remember to gather as much knowledge as you can, but be discerning. The more you understand, the more equipped you are. Whether it's learning about your spouse's illness, signing up for benefits, or preparing for what widowhood might feel like, do your homework. Ask questions, read, listen, and learn. Preparation won't erase the pain, but it might soften the blow, and that's something.

What you don't know can absolutely hurt you.

But what you *do* know? That just might carry you through.

CHAPTER 5

Humor Has a Space

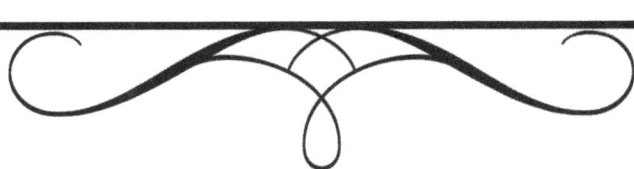

All widows who were present for long-term illnesses know how difficult it is to see their loved one fade away. After watching Jim decline for approximately 8 years – watching him lose his strength, ability to walk, and hold things – many lessons were learned. I believe the ones we learned and witnessed during those last couple of months were the most intense.

When the rest of the world and even the doctors acted like all was lost, I would look at my Jim and still see that he was in there. It seemed as if the hospital staff almost expected us to give up on him or fall into true despair at the loss of our loved one, but I learned that that reaction helps no one.

Having the strength of my family by my side and still seeing that my husband was in there, I refused to become the textbook Woman in Despair. So I chose otherwise. I learned that it was okay to cry, to laugh, and to be present. We laughed in front of him, we cried in front of him, we sang, but we included him in everything, and it made a difference not only to us, but to him as well.

During one of Jim's hospital stays, a nurse who clearly hadn't read his chart came in and started asking questions - something Jim absolutely despised. I was always there to be his buffer, to handle the interrogations that made him uncomfortable. This particular nurse was pressing him about his eye (there was nothing wrong with his eye), and Jim, with his trademark dry wit, suddenly looked at her and said, "Maybe I should take it out," while raising his hand as if he might literally remove his eye right then and there.

Lindsey and I stood by the side, trying to hold back our laughter, watching the nurse process what she'd just heard. She was completely caught off guard, unsure how to respond to Jim's unexpected and absurd comment.

Despite the serious circumstances of his illness, we were able to find a moment of humor. Jim's ability to deflect uncomfortable situations with sharp, unexpected comedy was his way of maintaining control and dignity, and in truth, we all needed that.

This was a huge lesson for me, even in the most challenging moments; there's room for laughter. There has to be. We couldn't let the heaviness of his illness consume us. By staying present and finding humor, we kept our spirits up and, more importantly, helped Jim feel like himself, not just a patient, but a person with a vibrant personality.

Moments like these continued to appear.

Before Jim coded and was given the breathing tube, he was vocal about his hatred for this. After nearly two weeks, the doctors told us that either the tube would be removed or a tracheotomy would be performed. They told us Jim would likely only survive a few hours after removing the breathing tube, but we knew that's what he wanted. He had always said he didn't want to be kept alive on machines, existing as a "vegetable." With heavy hearts, my children and I made the difficult decision to have the tube removed.

As they let us back into the room after the doctors removed it, we continued talking to Jim, asking questions even when we weren't sure he could respond. It was our way of staying connected and keeping hope alive. When we asked how he felt, his raspy voice surprised us all: "Better, no tube." The room full of doctors and nurses and the rest of our family fell silent, everyone's eyes darting to each other in disbelief.

We pressed on, asking if he was in pain. His response was quintessential Jim, "My butt," complaining about the bedsores that bothered him more than his numerous medical challenges. His wit and his spirit were still very much alive.

Don't get me wrong, it certainly wasn't easy finding humor in the darkest time of our lives, but we had to.

There were times when being all together in the ICU room got to be a lot. I remember when my sister, Debby, was visiting from Chicago, and Jimmy, Lindsey, Debby, and I were in the room with Jim. Though I can't recall exactly what it was, a funny comment set us off, and we started laughing, poking fun at each other, and just acting silly. We were doubled over in laughter and couldn't stop. That is, until we got this very serious look from Jimmy that, without words, said, "Stop it. Don't you realize you're in a hospital with sick people?" Mr. Logical crashed our silliness with that one look. The look reminded me of one that my Grandma Cassie would give to all the grandkids when we got to be a little too rambunctious on the Holidays and all she had to do was give us that look and say, "Children," and we quieted down immediately.

As I think back on that moment, I believe we were embarrassing Jimmy. He was clearly in no mood to be silly with us and perhaps didn't know what to make of it all, so we respected his wishes and calmed down. Laughing and being silly was our way of dealing with stress, but not his.

It's important to remember that each person must go through this journey their own way. It may be laughter; it may be tears; it may be retreating into solitude, but there is no right or wrong. We must allow each person to deal with the situation in a way that is right for them, even if you're processing things differently.

Jimmy is very private, much like his Dad, and this may have played into his response. We were in no way intentionally showing disrespect to Jim or to Jimmy, yet it still rubbed him the wrong way.

Despite our differences in coping mechanisms, the thing that was constant for all of us was our commitment to being present.

We have pictures of us sitting in the recliners they provided us, one on each side of the bed. We surrounded Jim's bed so that one of us could constantly have a reassuring hand on him to let him know we were there. If we got tired, we just put a pillow on the railing of the bed and put our head on it. Whether it was one of us there, or two or three, we made sure we were present.

Sophia drew many pictures and cards for her PaPa. They were taped to the walls where he could see them. Each new one she sent with us brought a reaction of some kind from Jim, letting us know he saw it; whether it was a little twitch at the side of his mouth, which we knew was a smile, or the blinking of his eyes, he let us know he was present and aware.

I wish the nurses and doctors could tell us what they saw in that room and what stuck in their memories. I hope what stayed with them long after we all left was Love, Family, Hope, Support, and Caring. Jim's primary care doctor, Dr. Vladimir, visited with his two assistants, Jackie and Christina (whom Jim loved to give a hard time whenever she had to ask all the questions and take his vitals before he saw the doctor) and sat with us for about 20 minutes, talking about what a pleasure it was to know and serve him. We were honored by that visit because we knew they must have had to do it during their lunchtime. We laughed with them about how every time they asked him, "How is he doing?" during his normal doctor visits over the years, he would always say "fine". It became a joke with all of us. Even with his sullen, sober face, he could always bring a smile to someone else.

This all might sound strange, finding humor during dark moments, but as you journey through widowhood, this may be one of your saving graces. Finding humor and lightheartedness may not come naturally, but that's okay! Lean on the strength of your family, be intentional in allowing those small, silly moments to bring a smile to your face, and remind your loved ones that the spirit can never be broken.

CHAPTER 6

Silence Is Golden

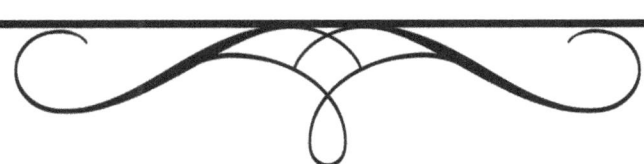

There are people in your life who you just know are there for you. I pray you have one. For me, that person is my sister, Debby. She's my baby sister, and it has always been just her and me. She lives all the way out in the Chicago suburbs, about 1,800 miles away, but when one of us needs the other, we don't hesitate. At the drop of a pin, we're on a plane.

Deb had been scheduled to fly to California for Penelope's baby shower, but as the day got closer, it became clear that God had other plans. She arrived in time to spend precious days with the Big Guy. She sat with us at the hospital, offering this quiet strength that gave the kids permission to take a break. I think they felt like they had to be there for me, but when Aunt Deb showed up, they could breathe a little.

We did take a break to go to the baby shower and celebrate Sophia's upcoming baby sister, but truthfully, our hearts weren't there. Everything felt heavy. We went through the motions, but we were carrying so much.

Deb would make sure we took turns eating, even when I didn't feel like it. She especially made me walk with her to the VA cafeteria to grab something healthy, eat it there instead of in the room, so we could go back and face whatever was waiting for us in that ICU room. That cafeteria made the best fresh salads, and we'd always split a large one and grab some sushi on the side. It became a ritual of sorts that allowed things to be simple, steady, and nourishing in a time when nothing else felt that way.

She didn't say much, but she exuded this quiet authority of tough love, but gentle. She had been through this before with Henryk, and you could tell. She knew what questions to ask and she noticed what others didn't. At the end of visiting hours, she would gently pull me away from Jim's bedside and take me back to her hotel room. She knew I needed to disconnect, to rest, to just stop for a moment, and she made me finally sleep.

The next morning, while I was still trying to piece myself together, she'd already be downstairs grabbing breakfast. She'd come back with a hot cup of tea and sit with me while I slowly got ready to go back. She never pushed. She just sat with me, and that quiet presence gave me the strength I didn't know I needed.

Her love reminded me of God's love; unconditional, steady, and unshakable. She never judged the choices I made or how I handled things. She just held me up.

Jim noticed her, too. Even in the thick of everything, he acknowledged she was there, and that meant something.

Deb left on a Tuesday. That Saturday morning, I called her ready to deliver the news I never wanted to say out loud, but she didn't answer. What I didn't know was that she, herself, was sitting in the ER. Back in Chicago, she'd slipped on the ice on her back porch. It was November, and winter had already hit hard. Her kneecap was shattered. When she called back later, she told me she wouldn't be able to attend any of Jim's services. She had surgery, then physical therapy, and thankfully, she's doing well now, but I know it broke her heart not to be there.

Still, her presence during those last days, those quiet moments in the cafeteria, in the hotel, and in the waiting room, was a gift I'll never forget.

That following spring, I flew out to Chicago to see her. We sat silently out on her beautiful back patio, just the two of us. In that quiet moment, with the comfort of my sister, the tears came. It was the first really good cry I'd had. Not a loud, gut-wrenching sob, just a gentle release that I didn't realize I needed. The tears had been locked inside me for so long, and in that space surrounded by her love, her understanding, and her quiet presence, I could finally let them go.

No judgment. No conversation needed. Just peace.

There's a kind of peace that only comes from being in the presence of someone who truly knows you, who doesn't ask for anything, and who doesn't try to fix it. They're just *there* where you need them to be, and that kind of silence is healing.

Find that quiet place for yourself. Maybe it's with a person like my sister, or maybe it's sitting on the beach, listening to the waves roll in. Our dentist's office is about two blocks away from the ocean. Several times after my appointment, I have walked over there and just sat without looking at a clock and stayed until I felt at peace. It refreshes me and seems to wash away the sadness. Maybe it's your favorite trail, or a special chair in your home, or even the bench where you and your spouse used to sit together. In that space, you just might find the strength to let go just a little.

Silence can be golden, and sometimes, it's exactly what your soul needs.

CHAPTER 7

Pomp and Circumstance

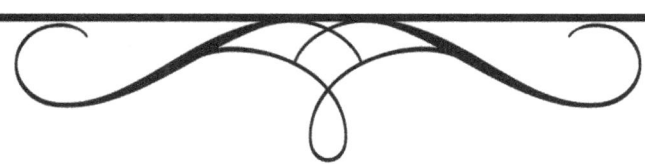

For a while, the funeral service had felt like it was the final chapter. It didn't necessarily feel like the end of grief or the end of healing, but like the closing of one part of the journey. It felt like something had finally come full circle. After all the hospital visits, paperwork, and whispered prayers, this was the day we handed Jim back to the world with honor and with love.

Truth be told, planning a funeral is exhausting, emotionally, physically, and mentally. Yet, somehow, the small details that you tend to overlook in the moment stick around in your memory after it's all said and done. Strange thoughts will hit you out of nowhere, things you'd never imagine yourself thinking in everyday life. Like when I went to pick out clothes for Jim to wear. Because of the amputation on one leg, I stood there, frozen, wondering, "Do I bring one shoe? Or two?" Funny enough, even with all of that overthinking, I ended up forgetting to include socks altogether! You would think that a silly moment like that would be quite memorable, but the truth is, I'd completely forgotten it occurred until I began pulling stories and memories for this book.

That's the thing about planning a funeral: it can feel like you're merely going through the motions and are navigating on autopilot. Dealing with the slew of emotions, being forced to make decisions, and still processing both minor and major details, it's a lot to ask your brain to also retain the memory of it all.

What I was fully aware of, however, were those small decisions we made that allowed us to keep Jim's memory alive and our love for him solid. The socks ultimately didn't matter, but some things did, like Jim's favorite ceramic dog, Buddy, whom we placed in the casket with him. Buddy had been his companion for years. The real Buddy passed before Jim did, but we kept the little statue around as a reminder. It even had a broken paw, just like Jim. It felt right to send it with him. It was important to us to get those small details right.

God showed up in quiet ways during those days.

On the way to the cemetery, I remember noticing a huge American flag flying high beside the freeway. Later, we learned it was the very first day that the flag had flown, and the land it stood on had just been dedicated to veterans. It might even become another resting place for heroes someday. That felt like more than a coincidence but rather a sign that Jim still fully mattered.

Because Jim was an honorably discharged veteran, he was buried at Riverside National Cemetery, and the funeral home walked us through every step. They were so kind and gentle, making the whole process easy to get through. Jim received full military honors: the folding of the flag, the presentation to me, the playing of TAPS, and the three-gun salute that pierced the silence and went straight through my soul.

Jim loved bagpipes. I don't know how that came to be, but the sound always stirred something in him. We found Tess, a local bagpiper, who helped us choose the songs and plan the flow of the ceremony. When she played, the sound carried on the wind, floating through every corner of that open space. It was somehow both haunting and beautiful.

Because of a connection with the local police department, Jim was given an escort during the procession, which was an unexpected honor. I'll never forget the feeling of seeing those officers, lights flashing, leading the way to his final resting place.

I quickly learned that you meet angels during this process and Tess was one of them. After the funeral, she told us to call her as soon as Jim's marker was placed. We did and it turned out she was available on his birthday. She came back and played "Happy Birthday" to him, along with a few other songs. She didn't have to but she did and baby Penelope, who was only about a month old by then, was able to be at her PaPa's celebration.

These and a handful of other moments from that day are crystal clear to me, while many others still feel like a blur. I found out much later that certain friends attended the funeral and I didn't even know they were there. Years later, at another funeral, a woman I knew casually told me she had been there. I was stunned. Not only was I shocked that she was there and I didn't know, but I was touched to learn that Jim had impacted more lives than I realized.

I spoke a few words at the service; just a thank you to everyone who had come to honor him. I kept it short. Jim wasn't a "churchy" guy, so I didn't want a traditional sermon and I asked a friend to speak instead. It was simple, heartfelt, and perfect.

One of the most surprising and memorable moments came from Sophia. As she walked with her dad toward the pavilion where the casket was being carried, she looked up and asked, "Daddy, is Nana going to get married again?" My son paused and gently replied, "I don't know, Sophia. I don't think that's what's on Nana's mind right now. She's still thinking about PaPa."

Children say the most unexpected things that catch you off guard with their innocence and clarity. She had already registered in her mind that PaPa was gone, and her little heart was wondering what came next. I hadn't even gone that far in my own mind.

There's a picture of her from that day, standing quietly at the short wall near the burial site, watching. She was all alone in that moment, just observing. I often wonder what was going through her mind. I may never know, but I'll never forget the image.

After the ceremony, we were invited to see the actual site where Jim was being buried. That part felt strange in a way, but also intimate. It made the staff at the cemetery seem so human. They treated the process with such dignity and care. Watching them lower the casket, seeing how gently they worked, meant more than words could say.

I believe the ceremony was fitting for Jim. He never sought recognition for his service. In fact, he didn't even want his medals when we offered to reorder them after learning they'd been stolen. "What do I want those for?" he said. He'd made his peace with that part of his past. But in his later years, when people thanked him for his service, he began to accept it with a quiet nod. I think, in his heart, he knew it mattered. We ended up ordering the medals anyway after he was gone, and they are next to the frame with his flag in it.

The ceremony gave him the honor he never asked for, but deserved.

For me, it brought a quiet kind of closure. It didn't fix the grief or erase the pain, but it created a line in time: a before and after. Once the ceremony was over, I could start thinking, just a little, about tomorrow and what it would mean to live again. Even something as small as going out to McDonald's with a friend felt like a first step and a change in routine. This was going to be a new rhythm to my life and something I had to get used to.

If you are in the middle of it all as you read this book, I want you to take a moment and pause. Instead of continuing to move on autopilot, allow yourself to take in the small moments around you. If you can, journal the details or situations that stand out for you. Perhaps it's a list of those who were at the funeral or maybe it's notes on the kind things family, friends, or neighbors said or did for you. Later, you may come to appreciate having a record of this moment that you can look back on.

Remember, after the pomp and circumstance settles, so does something in you. You'll feel that soft shift signaling that while the chapter is closed, the book isn't finished, not quite yet.

CHAPTER 8
We All Have Limits

One of the biggest lessons I learned the hard way was to only do what you can.

I know that sounds like common knowledge, but when so much of your life is focused on doing for others, when you and your family experience the loss of a loved one, you may find yourself continuing to ensure that you are available for them in whatever they may need.

It sounds good, but I had to remind myself that I, too, am grieving. Attempting to overextend myself in my own time of need is a one-way ticket to burnout and broken commitments.

It was a true struggle to simply say "I can't."

For months on end, after Jim's passing, I was being invited to coffees, dinners, lunches, events, and so many other outings that would have consumed my time and energy. I knew why. These were friends, families, and colleagues who thought it was best for me to get out and be around others. They believed that my being "cooped up" at home was bad for me, and in order to heal, I had to be out and about.

That couldn't be further from the truth, but I could not bring myself to say so. So… I accepted just about every invitation that was sent my way. Why wouldn't I? They all cared about me and wanted the best for me. Maybe it was also their way of grieving

Jim. Whatever the reason, I felt obligated to say yes as often as I could.

The truth of the matter was, I had little energy to get up and go anywhere. It wasn't because I was broken or deeply depressed. Sure, I was sad, but I believe my body needed time to adapt to the new life I was going to have to get used to. All I wanted to do was sleep and not be bothered. It was like my brain was aware of this need, too. I struggled to focus at times and would find myself zoning out or completely blanking.

It came to a point that, even though I accepted the invitations, I would later have to back out or break the commitment completely, simply because my body and brain would not allow me to get going.

We may hate to admit it, but there may be some days when you have made commitments, and there is no way you can show up. It's often better to break a commitment than it is to injure yourself either physically or mentally to keep up appearances. Remember, many of your invites may come from a space of love and care and they may simply want what's best for you. Don't be afraid to explain what that is. You can even explain to people that you are having a rough day and why, and they will most likely understand.

I went to so many outings and events that I was scheduled for and once I arrived, I deeply wondered why I was there at all. I couldn't concentrate and I didn't want to be around groups of people. I most certainly wasn't interested in what others were interested in. It'd been a continuous waste of time.

Had I expressed my inability to attend, not only would I have received love and support from those who invited me, but I would have given myself the space and time I needed to continue to heal.

This isn't to say that I would have rejected all invites, but I would have been much more discerning. Remember to do this for yourself. Don't be afraid to say no when you need to and to only do what you know you can.

I personally found that much of my healing was done alone or with family. We went through boxes that were stored in the garage and I told stories about who Jim and I were back when the kids were too young to remember. Those moments truly aided in my healing and were the only thing I needed. No outing, no groups, just me and my family sharing memories.

I found that the arrival of our second granddaughter, Penelope, also aided in my healing. She was born about six weeks after Jim passed and brought such a fresh perspective to our lives at a much-needed time. Penelope did not get a chance to meet her

PaPa, but Sophia promised that she would make sure that PJ knew who he was. Ironically, PJ looks just like Jim. Several people have seen pictures of her and say the resemblance between her and Jim is uncanny. From the first day she came home from the hospital, I could stare into her eyes and she would stare back, and those eyes belonged to Jim. She points up when asked about PaPa, and connects him to the Moon and the heavens. I guess they are synonymous in her mind. Her arrival was an unexpected, but much-needed, event that I will forever cherish.

Knowing what I can handle has allowed me to keep my sanity and protect my peace when I needed it the most, but I most certainly learned the hard way.

There was the time after Jim passed, when I was cleaning the house, getting it ready to sell. I made the decision to sell about a year after he was gone and was trying to get everything in order. I was up on a stepstool cleaning out the pantry when I lost my balance. I fell hard, first onto the kitchen island and then to the floor. I was alone and the house was quiet. I looked down and saw blood on the brand-new floors and my first thought was, "Oh no, I just ruined the new floor," and tried to wipe it up with my sleeve. When I was able, I crawled, in pain, to Jim's chair. Once I made it there, I stayed. There was water nearby and I'd eaten recently, so I told myself I'd be okay until the kids came the next morning.

I called Jimmy and let him know what happened, but I insisted he didn't need to come. I didn't want to be a burden and I didn't want to make a fuss. Later, I found out I had fractured my pelvis in two places. If I'd let someone come sooner, maybe they would've realized how bad it was and maybe I wouldn't have spent the night in pain, convincing myself I was fine.

I know it sounds silly now, as I look back on it, but I was so in my head about not being a burden to someone that I allowed myself to be hurt and in pain. It turns out, being selfish, especially in moments of healing through grief, is essential.

That's what grief and pride can do; they convince you that you're strong enough to handle it alone or even that you should handle it alone, but you shouldn't. No one should.

Do only what you can handle each day. If your body says I'm just too tired to get out of bed, allow yourself the grace to listen to it and relax and heal. Some days, the adrenaline will be flowing and you will feel like you can accomplish so much, while the next day may feel like a letdown and you accomplish nothing. Take the roller coaster ride in stride and enjoy its high points but do not get stuck in the deep valleys. Most importantly, get help if you need it.

You might be surrounded by people who love you, but they don't always know how to help. They may even be grieving, too. They may also be watching someone they love decline and they don't know what to do with their hands or their hearts. But if you open the door and let them in, they will rise to the occasion, not just for your sake but for theirs too.

CHAPTER 9

The Power of "Normal"

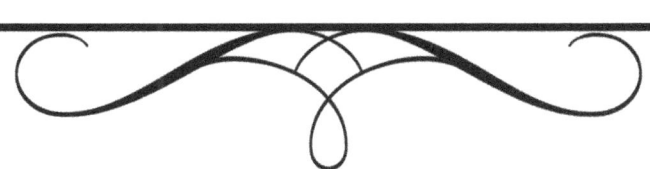

The first few weeks after Jim passed almost felt... normal. At least, that's what I told myself. No more hospital visits, no more late-night calls from the nurses, no more gowns, gloves, and masks. Then the silence settled in, and I realized that this wasn't normal at all. It was just the absence of chaos.

It reminded me of the pandemic. Remember how we all kept saying we wanted life to go "back to normal," but when we finally got there, it didn't look anything like the life we remembered? That's how widowhood felt. What once was normal had vanished and now, I had to figure out what came next.

If your spouse has or is experiencing a long-term illness, then I don't have to tell you...those long hospital days are hard. Not just physically, but mentally and emotionally. During the last six months of Jim's life, I began to realize just how important it was to let family and even friends be involved. You can't do this kind of thing alone. You might think you can or you might even try, but caregiving, especially when you're not sure what the outcome will be, can take everything out of you.

At first, I tried to keep things as normal as I could. I kept holding my Monday night Mary Kay meetings on Zoom, trying to hold onto that part of my life. Eventually, it became too much and I just couldn't keep up. I was so thankful when the core women in my unit stepped up. Karyn started running the meetings, Valerie (who has since passed) did recognition, Diana shared product info and training, and Alma (who also recently passed) or Patty would end with something inspirational. I would pop in when I could, just to wave and say hi, and every time, they'd cheer like I was the guest of honor. It gave me something to look forward to when so much of life felt uncertain.

There were hospital stays where I was the only one allowed in because of COVID protocols. Jim would sleep a lot (he was on Dilaudid or Fentanyl at times) but he still hated that he couldn't be more present. I remember him apologizing once for sleeping so much. We told him, "That's what helps you heal." He grinned and said, "Well, guess I'm going to be a whole lot better soon."

For so long, going to the hospital was my daily routine. I even remember one day I had a tooth pulled, and by 1 p.m., Jim was already calling to ask where I was. One of the kids had gone to visit him, but he was used to me being there every single day without fail. He could hear my footsteps coming down the hall. I'd have a minute or two to prepare myself for any new update while I suited up with my isolation gown, gloves, and mask. One time, he even asked why it took me so long to get into the room.

I stayed busy during those visits, reading, texting updates to family and friends, trying to keep up with clients who had no idea I was sitting in a hospital room, wondering if my husband was going to live or die. I know it helped Jim to have me there. I could explain what the nurses were doing, advocate for him, and ask questions he didn't have the energy to ask. I was his voice so much of the time that that became my way of life.

But little by little, reality set in. With Jim gone, life was no longer normal and it wasn't going back to how it was.

When he passed, I went straight into motion. At first, I kept busy, because that's what I do: clearing out the house, going through drawers, cabinets, the pantry, sorting medications, organizing paperwork, and doing the physical labor of moving forward. It wasn't that I was cold or detached… it was simply survival. Physical movement became my release. This may have come from being with my sister after Henryk's death. He was a smoker, and every room was saturated with smoke. We opened the windows, washed the walls, scrubbed the carpet, and removed anything we could that smelled like that. Her poor dogs weren't sure what was going on, but then came the fun of shopping for a new couch, end tables, and more. I was so glad to be able to be there for her during those days, never knowing how similar our lives would be. Now it was my turn to do the same.

There were days I'd walk into a store and catch myself putting things in the cart that *he* liked, not me. I'd pick up the phone to tell him something funny Sophia had said or to ask about a bill or a show he liked. Habits don't die when someone does. They linger.

I split my time between home and the kids' house. I'd spend two days at my house to take care of the cats, then go back to the kids and stay with them the rest of the week. That back-and-forth helped me ease into the shift without feeling completely uprooted. Eventually, after about a year, I made the decision to sell the house. That was a huge step. It wasn't just the home we shared. We looked for a single-story home with a small backyard that didn't need much upkeep, and we found it. It came with a VA mortgage rate of 2.5%, which was unheard of. I could have stayed, financially and emotionally. But I knew it was time.

Truthfully, I think God had prepared me. Jim had been away from home so much during those final months that I'd already started adjusting to being there without him.

Selling the house wasn't easy. The first offer fell through, so the process dragged on for six months. I found a picture of Jimmy, Sophia, and me standing in the emptiness of the open area once it was finally cleared out. I saw that photo, and it hit me—we were really moving on. Sophia spent a lot of her young years coming to our house.

I didn't move in alone. I had a conversation with Lindsey about finding a place together. With Sophia and the new baby, Jimmy's house was getting full. It was time for all of us to create space. We found a place, a cute little rental we jokingly called the "buggy house" because, well, it was. After three months of battling bugs, we knew we needed something better.

Eventually, we found the place we're in now. It wasn't available until June 1st, so we rented a tiny Airbnb for a few weeks. Just the basics, but perfect. We had room for the dogs, the cats, and each other. Once we moved into our new home, something shifted. I started leaning into life again.

I started visiting churches, joined a women's Bible study group, and got myself involved in a local networking group. I even hired a life coach. She helped me realize that, little by little, I was stepping into something new. Something good.

I started doing more with Mary Kay again. Jim had always told me to keep going with it and that it mattered to me and that it brought me joy. After his death, I held onto that advice and focused on doing what brought me joy. In August, I made the decision to step down as a director. I'd led about 50 women, but I no longer wanted to feel responsible for anyone else's growth or momentum. I didn't want to be a babysitter anymore. That decision hit me financially, but I haven't regretted it.

I'm still a consultant. I still get reorders, and I still book appointments when I want to. It's given me purpose, but more importantly, it's introduced me to new people, and that's been part of my healing too.

Maintaining normalcy doesn't mean trying to go back to what used to be. It means finding things that make me feel whole and like my true self. Mary Kay was that thing. Cleaning and rearranging was that thing. I keep finding more and more things and it keeps me and my life totally fulfilled and God has a way of sending more of those things my way.

For example, I had a situation where I invested some money and it didn't go well. I remember feeling that fear in the pit of my stomach. I would have normally leaned on Jim to feel better or to get advice on what to do next. Perhaps he would have even prevented the whole situation. But I didn't have him to save me from this situation. I had to deal with it on my own.

I called those I was investing with to ask for an explanation, but the man treated me like I was less than and even told me that maybe I should just take the loss on my taxes and close my account. I never felt so disrespected in my life.

Again, I felt the need to turn to Jim, but rather than sit and wallow in that feeling of stupidity, I embraced my new normal and decided to do something about it. I prayed to God for answers on how I could educate myself and not be so financially illiterate. God answered that prayer by sending a couple back into my life that I hadn't been in touch with for several years, and they were able to educate me. I am now in the Financial Services industry; Life Licensed in two states, and studying for my Securities License.

Did I ever think, at age 76, I would be able to kick my brain into a study mode again, go take a State test with a room full of much younger people, and pass that test on my first shot? No, but guess what, I did it! Now I am able to help others become more financially literate, debt-free, and retirement-ready, but most importantly, I have my new "thing" that fills my cup.

I went on a cruise recently. The ocean has always been my healing space. My safe place. I looked forward to the waves, the peace, the sun, and the stillness. This cruise was to honor Jim because it was something he wanted to do but we never got around to it. There was even a seagull that came and rested on my balcony railing and stayed there for at least five minutes. It kept staring into my eyes and made me wonder if maybe it was Jim saying he was glad I had done this and that he was here with me. Do I still need to heal? Of course. I probably always will, but this is part of it.

I've found a rhythm. I don't feel guilty if I want to stay in bed for a while. I sit outside in the sun with the dogs. I drink my tea. I take a breath. I don't owe anyone a schedule. I don't have to report in. That's a strange thing to adjust to after being a caregiver for so long, but it's freeing, too

When I go to visit my sister in Chicago, I don't have to be "on." We just sit together, watch the birds and squirrels from her patio, drink tea, and let the quiet hold us.

That's what creating a new normal has looked like for me. It hasn't been fast or perfect, but it's been real.

The same should be said for you. Remember who you were before the loss. Think back to before you were married, or early in the marriage. What were your dreams? What made you smile just because? Did you want to travel? Plant a garden? Start something new?

Go back to that. Revisit what brought you joy outside of your role as a wife, and build from there.

Your new normal is waiting. It won't look like the life you had before but it can still be beautiful.

CHAPTER 10

The 5 Stages of Widowhood

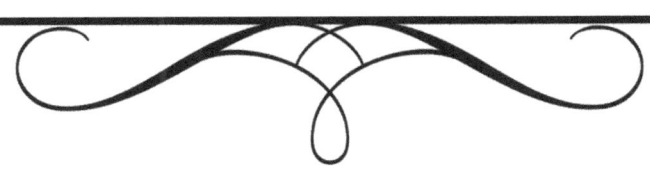

People like to talk about the five stages of grief: denial, anger, bargaining, depression, and acceptance.

I won't say those stages didn't exist for me; rather, they didn't match what I lived through.

I found that widowhood has its own rhythm, its own rise and fall. Going through it myself, I realized that my grief unfolded in a different way. After analyzing my journey, I created what I believe to be the five stages of widowhood: **Relief, Guilt, Numbness, Letting Go, and Rebuilding.**

They didn't come in a straight line, either. In truth, it was messy. Sometimes the stages overlapped or circled back when I least expected it. Even though it was a difficult journey to pass through, these stages served as mile markers on the road I never asked to be on.

In conversations with other widows, I have found that these stages were present in just about every scenario. For me, there's comfort in knowing what to expect and, even more so, knowing that I'm not the only one experiencing it.

My prayer is that by breaking down each of the stages, you will understand where you currently are in your journey and find solace in the fact that this is all part of a process that we experience together.

Stage One: RELIEF

The very first thing I felt when Jim passed was relief.

That may sound awful to someone who hasn't been there, but when you've watched someone you love suffer for so long, there's a part of you that's thankful their pain is over. I was relieved that the constant hospital visits were done, that I didn't have to hear the beeping machines or alarms alerting us that something was wrong, or sleep in those awful chairs that make your back ache. I was relieved that the endless "hurry up and wait" routine of the ICU was behind us.

Being a caregiver takes everything out of you. You run on fumes, and you don't even realize how heavy the weight is until it's gone.

When Jim took his last breath, I let out the deepest sigh of my life. It wasn't just sadness, though. It was as if I breathed out every sleepless night, every worried phone call, every moment of watching him hurt. All of it left my body in that one breath.

If you've been a caregiver, you know exactly what I'm talking about. If you haven't, know this: relief is not the same as wanting them gone. It's the body's way of saying, "You can rest now."

This phase came upon me quickly. I could feel the tiredness and hopelessness drain from my body. I found that it was simpler to wake up in the morning without a weight hanging over me, without asking, "What pain do I have to deal with today?" I could finally wake up and make my own decisions.

Stage Two: GUILT

The relief didn't last long before the guilt set in.

I felt guilty for not having to organize his medications anymore. I felt guilty for sleeping through the night without getting up to check on him. I even felt guilty for walking out the door without making sure someone was there to stay with him.

It's a cruel thing, finally having the freedom you begged God for during the hardest days, only to feel ashamed for having it. The so-called "freedom" felt foreign and, in a way, unjustified.

I remember thinking, *Does this mean I didn't love him enough? Does this make me a bad wife?*

But here's what I've learned: feeling relief when someone's suffering ends doesn't erase the love you had for them. It just means you were there for all of it, and you gave so much of yourself that your body is now trying to recover. Guilt is just love in a different form; it's proof that you cared so deeply.

Stage Three: NUMBNESS

After guilt came numbness.

I wasn't falling apart every day, but I wasn't fully living either. I could go through the motions of cooking, cleaning, and watching the grandkids, but I wasn't really *there*.

During this stage, I started sorting through Jim's things. I didn't do it all at once. I'd pick one drawer or one shelf, and if I got overwhelmed, I would stop and find myself staring off into the distance.

Sometimes I'd pull out one of his shirts and just stand there holding it, breathing in whatever faint scent still lingered. There weren't any tears and I had no visible reaction, but I could still feel the ache in my chest. Yet, there were days when the ache seemed to disappear, too, and the guilt would set back in as if I was wrong for not crying that day.

The battle between guilt and numbness ensued. One day, I'm numb and feel nothing, the next I'm angry that I felt nothing the day before.

When I finally began to analyze my emotions, I began to realize that the numbness was my mind's way of protecting me. It gave me space to adjust before I had to face the deeper waves of grief. Soon, the guilt disappeared as I allowed the numbness to do its job.

If you're here now, I want you to know that being numb doesn't mean you're not grieving. It means your heart is pacing itself.

Stage Four: LETTING GO

Letting go is one of the hardest things you can do as a widow. Sometimes it feels like you're attempting to erase or forget about your loved one. This was a toxic thought that appeared one too many times in my grieving.

One of the hardest things I had to let go of was Jim's project truck, a 1942 Chevy pickup truck.

That truck had been his baby. I can still picture him standing out there in the driveway, wiping his hands on a rag, and tinkering under the hood.

Selling it felt like I was betraying him.

But there came a point when I realized I was holding onto the truck for him, and not for the kids or me. It was a memory that had a physical entity.

When we first bought that truck about 20 years ago, Jim tinkered with it until he got it running and came into the house and said, "C'mon". I had no idea what was going on. He had me jump into the passenger seat, he turned the key, and we took a quick drive through the neighborhood.

Was it pretty? No. But we could see how beautiful it would be once he restored it back to its original glory. Several people waved at us and gave us a thumbs-up. One "older" man actually waved us down and he and Jim talked about the truck and what it could be.

When I went to meet Gil (a friend's husband who purchased it after Jim passed) at the yard where it was stored, I couldn't even stay to watch it be removed from its parking space and loaded on the trailer.

Letting go didn't mean I loved him any less, and if he could've spoken to me in that moment, I think he would've said, "Let it go, Sam. Don't let a hunk of metal keep you from moving forward." It meant I was finally making space for the next part of my life, mentally and financially.

Letting go of items, habits, and unnecessary tasks that no longer fit into the new life you will rebuild is essential. It doesn't have to feel like an erasure of what once was. Instead, give honor to your loved one, their things, and your old way of life by gently letting go of the old and making way for the new.

Stage Five: REBUILDING

Once you've found the strength to let go of what was, you can now begin to rebuild for what is to come.

Rebuilding didn't start with some big moment. It was slow and quiet.

It began with saying yes to lunch with friends. Then I signed up for things that had nothing to do with being a wife or widow, but rather, things that were just for me.

Little by little, I began to see myself again, not just as "Jim's widow," but as Sandie; daughter, sister, mother, grandmother, friend, businesswoman.

I laughed again without feeling bad about it. I soon began making plans without that feeling of dread. Then, one day, I caught myself watching the sun rise and thinking, *That's beautiful.*

That's when I knew I was rebuilding.

Don't get me wrong, I love my husband and I always will. I would much rather have him by my side, but that's out of my control. I know that he would want me to honor him and move on and continue my life.

The truth is, I'm trying. Even after nearly three years without him, I'm still trying. Holidays are hard. Songs still pop up that make me cry and choke up. A picture of him during his healthier days sometimes appears in my Facebook memories, and my heart skips a beat.

But instead of allowing the pain to linger, I allow myself to enjoy the happy memories we have from the 51 years of marriage and the outcome of our union: a wonderful son, a beautiful daughter, and two granddaughters to carry on his memory.

Understanding these five stages didn't "fix" my grief but they gave me a map when the ground felt shaky.

If you're currently going through these stages, know this: you'll move through each stage in your own time and in your own way. You might jump around, skip one, or circle back to another and that's okay.

Just keep going, because one day, without even realizing it, you'll be standing in the light again, holding your grief in one hand and your new life in the other, a*nd both will belong to you.*

CHAPTER 11
Final Words

As you come to the end of this book, I'd like to leave you with these words: You are not alone. You are loved. Your life still matters. As you head back to your new normal and begin rebuilding, do it at your own pace. Listen to your body and your soul, and remember that you are the one making your decisions now. Stand firm and make them. Will you make mistakes? Of course, but use them as learning experiences to expand your life.

Here are some helpful tips and resources that I wish had been shared with me when I first began this journey. Please do your own research and use your discernment to create the best support system for you.

There are many people and organizations out there that want to help you through this; you just need to reach out and find them. And sometimes, you have to ask more than once.

TIPS

For Military Wives:

During the hospitalization times at the VA, the doctors and staff members were very good about directing us to where we could find information. After Jim passed, I received a large Manila envelope, and in it were various brochures and pamphlets that let me know what I could expect at 3 months, 6 months, and a year.

Unfortunately, they were very generic, and at the time, I was overwhelmed with forms to submit to get funeral benefits, survivor compensation, and anything else that was available for Jim. It felt like grief on one side of the room and paperwork on the other, and I was expected to keep walking back and forth between the two like it was normal.

Dealing with the VA involves so much red tape, though, and if your loved one is a veteran, my strongest suggestion is this: **do not try to walk that maze alone.** Find a VSO (Veteran Service Officer), the American Legion, or the VFW to help walk you through the process. Each organization has at least one person whose job is to help survivors navigate this maze. Let them do what they are trained to do. Let them help you.

For Those Dealing with Hospice:

I was astounded at how much Hospice was able to help and take the "what do I do now" away from us as a family.

Once the representative came and confirmed what we already believed in our hearts, he asked us very simple questions, and those simple questions set everything in motion. He helped set up the funeral home, made the arrangements for the removal of the body, and explained what we could expect in the next few days.

They also arranged for the removal of the hospital bed that was sitting there in the front room. I don't think I could have brought myself to do that, so having their support meant the world to me.

I will never forget that part, because it's one thing to know someone is gone. It is another thing to look at an empty bed where they fought so hard to stay.

If Hospice is involved for your family, let them carry what they can carry. You have enough.

For Those with Home Health Nurses:

During the different times when we had home health care nurses, we learned a lot. These nurses need to be versed in all kinds of medical issues, and sometimes their personalities were not matched with the work they had to do. Just like sometimes you'd get a doctor that didn't seem to care about what he said or how it affected the family.

We became very hands-on with Jim, with the approval of the doctors and hospitals.

I was taught how to treat an open wound after the first amputation of three toes until the wound vac came. Did I ever think I would be able to stomach doing that? No. But once I was trained, it was no big deal.

Lindsey and I were taught how to administer "ball" antibiotics through a PICC line and learned the proper procedures for sterilization of our hands, the IV line and ports, and the attaching of the "ball" of antibiotics that would shrivel up as they were delivered into Jim's bloodstream.

I'm sharing that because some of what you'll be asked to do may surprise you, and you may just surprise yourself. You might feel like, *I can't do this,* at first, but you will do it anyway, because love makes you brave in ways you can't imagine.

Also, if something does not feel right, speak up. Ask the question again, request clarity, request training, and request help. This is not the time to pretend you understand something if you do not. Your loved one's care depends on you being willing to say, "Stop. Explain that again."

For Those With Local Support:

I remember a time when I had to knock on neighbors' doors until I found someone home who could help.

Jim was too weak to get into the car from the wheelchair and I couldn't lift him. I didn't know them well, but I had no choice.

A man whom I had seen walking his dog earlier came out and helped. He practically lifted Jim into the car himself.

That day, I drove him all the way to the VA. When we got there, the nurse took one look at him and said, "You're not going to any appointment. He's going straight to the ER."

That help made all the difference, but I had to ask for it. I had to put pride aside and just ask.

So if I can give you a simple, plain piece of advice from that day, it's this: do not wait until you are desperate to let someone help you. Ask. Ask while you can still breathe. Ask while you can still think. Ask before you hit the wall.

Resources

1. **Veteran Service Officer (VSO), American Legion, and VFW**

   If your loved one is a veteran, do not try to navigate VA benefits alone. These organizations often have someone whose job is to help survivors walk through the maze of paperwork and red tape.

2. **VA Bereavement Counseling (Vet Centers)**

   If you are a surviving spouse, child, or parent, you may qualify for grief counseling through VA Vet Centers. It can help to talk with someone who understands the unique grief that can come with military service and service-connected illness.

3. **TAPS (Tragedy Assistance Program for Survivors)**

   TAPS provides peer support, resources, and grief care for those grieving a death in the military or veteran community. Knowing support was available 24/7 gave me comfort, even on days I did not use it.

4. **Vietnam Veterans' Wives & Surviving Spouses of Agent Orange (Facebook group)**

   This group sustained me because the advice is firsthand and the understanding is immediate. You have to request to join, but once you're in, you realize you're not alone and there is real knowledge being shared by women who have lived it.

5. **Vietnam Veterans of America (VVA)**

   VVA is focused on Vietnam-era veterans and also supports families through advocacy and local chapters. Local events and remembrance spaces can be meaningful when you need connection and community.

6. **Church-based Grief Recovery Groups**

   Many churches offer Biblically-based grief support groups. Even if you do not join long-term, sitting with people who can hold faith and grief in the same room can be a lifeline.

7. **A personal coach, counselor, or trusted guide**

   I worked with a personal life and business coach before and after Jim passed, and it helped me understand that my grief did not always look like other people's. Sometimes the most helpful support is someone who can help you make sense of your emotions without trying to rush you through them.

If you are a faith-driven person, be sure to lean on God for the ultimate support. My God was with me every step of the way, and I can look back and see Him at work.

From getting me used to being in our house by myself because Jim was in and out of hospitals so much, to letting the drive to my house to feed the cats be an escape for me where I didn't need to think or concentrate on the hospital and what was happening, to Jim being in hospitals continuously for almost the last 2 months of his life.

He was not normally at "home," whether it was ours or the kids', and I feel it was in preparation for what was to come.

I carry an angel in an organza pouch that was attached to Jim's bed during his last stay at the hospital, and we made sure that it traveled wherever he went, attached to his bed. I carry that angel with me in my purse every day as a reminder that angels will appear when we need them.

I never found out who put it there, but it meant so much to us and offered us so much comfort.

Resources will come from all areas. Just keep your eyes and ears open.

And again, **ASK** for information and use it.

Whether politically correct or not, I offer up this prayer for you.

Father, I ask Your healing on each person who reads my story. I pray that it will be as comforting to them as it was to me as I wrote it. Our love needs to be based on Your unconditional love for us. Let us realize that You are there for each one of us.

I pray that you, the reader, will feel the comfort of the peace that passeth understanding that God offers, for the rest of your life.

In Jesus' Name, Amen

Acknowledgments

So many people encouraged me throughout the writing of this book, in one shape or form.

To my kids, Jimmy and Lindsey, who knew I was writing a "book" but never interfered and allowed me to write it my way. When they read it, I hope they will be proud.

To my sister for being my sounding board at different times and supporting me in so many ways.

To John and Bonnie Calfa for always believing in me.

To the following people who supported me near the end when I didn't know if I was going to be able to finish this dream, in alphabetical order.

- Aimee Manly
- Anna Laguna
- Christy Johnson
- Cynthia Pleasant
- Dahlene Holliness
- Debra Hodges
- Dr. Catrina Elliott

- Florence Rivera Monzon
- Georgeen Whitney
- Jessica Hunter
- Latrice Jones
- Mercedita Noland
- Sandi Rowland
- Sandy Driver
- Stephanie and Antonio Ratliff
- Sue Nieto
- Teri Sue Parker

I would also like to thank Porsché Mysticque Steele, of MysticqueRose Publishing, for working with me and pulling out so many emotions and thoughts, and memories, through tearful sessions when the heart of this book was solidified. You helped me put my ideas together to make this book a reality, instead of just a dream.

And, last but not least, to my husband Jim, who shared so much of my life with me. Jim, I hope we did you proud and honored your wishes to the best of our ability. I miss you every day.

About the Author

Sandie Fuenty was born in a small town in Southern Illinois, known for its picturesque town square and close-knit community. Her family later relocated to the Chicago suburbs, where she spent her formative years before marrying and moving to California in 1980. Those early roots—grounded in family, faith, and resilience—continue to shape the woman she is today.

With a career spanning Corporate America and the construction industry, Sandie spent many years working in male-dominated fields, including more than three decades helping to build and operate a successful HVAC business alongside her husband. These experiences sharpened her professionalism, leadership skills, and deep understanding of what it means to remain confident and capable while staying true to one's femininity and beauty from the inside out.

After 32 years with Mary Kay, Sandie has become keenly aware of what she calls the "total package" of a woman: strength, grace, competence, and compassion. Her work today reflects that philosophy as she continues her Mary Kay business and serves others through financial services, helping individuals and families gain clarity, confidence, and education around their finances.

In November 2022, Sandie's husband of 51 years passed away after a long battle with health complications related to Agent Orange exposure during the Vietnam War. She walked beside him through his decline as a devoted caregiver, an experience that profoundly shaped her perspective on love, loss, and resilience. Today, she is intentionally creating a new chapter of life while helping care for her two granddaughters and remaining closely connected to her children in Orange County.

Active in her church, Bible study, and community organizations, Sandie also works with nonprofit initiatives and enjoys travel, especially trips back to the Chicago area to spend time with her sister. Known for her spontaneity, she can have her bags packed and ready to go within an hour. She is an Ambassador for the Mary Kay Ash Charitable Foundation, focused on finding a cure to end women's cancers and putting an end to domestic violence. When she's home, she treasures time with family, her dogs and cats, and making memories while fixing up her home alongside her daughter.

Sandie is an author, columnist, and avid reader who has been featured as a co-author in several bestselling anthologies, including *Greatness Is Your Journey, What's Your Why?, Catalyst #2, Rise Books 1 and 2, Diamonds of Wisdom,* and *Showing Up GSFE.*

'Til Death Do Us Part is her first solo book.

Sandie's life today is centered on encouraging others to continue pursuing life even in the midst of grief. Through her story, her work, and her unwavering faith, she offers hope, perspective, and reassurance that healing does not mean forgetting. It means moving forward with love.